21 WAYS
TO RAISE
FAST CASH

Quick Methods to Raise
Cash Online and Offline

By Mike Johnson
www.BlackHatSoftware.net

Disclaimer

This book has been written to provide information about Internet marketing. Every effort has been made to make this book as complete and accurate as possible. However, there may be mistakes in typography or content. Also, this e-book provides information on Internet marketing only up to the publishing date. Therefore, this ebook should be used as a guide - not as the ultimate source of Internet marketing information.

The purpose of this book is to educate. The author and the publisher does not warrant that the information contained in this e-book is fully complete and shall not be responsible for any errors or omissions. The author and publisher shall have neither liability nor responsibility to any person or entity with respect to any loss or damage caused or alleged to be caused directly or indirectly by this book.

About the Author

Mike Johnson is Former member of the US Army who Retired to find his fortune on the Internet. Mike found his pot of Gold with Affiliate and Internet Marketing and continues to forage for additional ways to Make Money Online.

Mike's Credit's Include several Marketing Titles, the very popular BlackHatSoftware.net blog, and his very popular Auto Blog Blueprint Membership site and Forums.

Mike's Expertise in Internet and Affiliate Marketing is recognized Worldwide and he is routinely mentioned among the best names in Online Marketing.

Table of Contents

Introduction   6

Method #1: Hold a Firesale   8

Method #2: Find a Freelance Tutoring Job   13

Method #3: Sell Junk Online   15

Method #4: Sell Crafts on Etsy   16

Method #5: Sell Your Own Special Reports   18

Method #6: Freelance as an Administrative Assistant   22

Method #7: Become a Freelance Writer   24

Method #8: Freelance Graphic Design Work   28

Method #9: Internet Marketing for Local Businesses   32

Method #10: Web Design Work   35

Method #11: Put an Advertisement on Your Car   37

Method #12: Self Publishing   38

Method #13: Find a Freelance Babysitting Job   42

Method #14: Use Myspace Forums to Sell Products   44

Method #15: Use Twitter & Myspace Forum   47

Method #16: Enter into a Joint Venture Partnership   49

Method #17: Offer Services to Internet Marketers   50

Method #18: Offer a Special Offer   51

Method #19: Sell Custom Content Mini-Sites   52

Method #20: Make a 5/95 JV Offer   52

Method #21: Sell Unprofitable Parts of Your Business   53

Conclusion   55

Resources   56

Introduction

Let me start by saying what this guide is not. It is not:

> * A list of "get rich quick" schemes
>
> * A guide to participating in pyramid schemes
>
> * A list of multi-level marketing schemes
>
> * A list of business opportunities
>
> * A guide for creating a successful business in the long term
>
> * An attempt to get you to sell my products as an affiliate

That's right: unlike virtually all of the other guides you'll find on the Internet about making money fast, this one won't tell you to do it through questionable, unreasonable strategies; or through a business opportunity that will incur a loss in the short run.

In fact, this guide is the opposite of that. It focuses on how you can make money in the short run--legally, and by using reasonable, easy-to-follow methods. It won't tell you to incur losses, to make large investments up front, or to be patient.

This guide is designed for people like you: people who need money now; and can't wait for some business opportunity to work itself out.

With that said, let's get into the substantive content. In the next 21 mini-chapters, I'm going to tell you how you can make money online and offline in a short amount of time and without risking any large investments in the process.

Method #1: Hold a Firesale

If you've been involved in Internet business for several years, you've probably seen your fair share of firesales. Some companies do it before going out of business; while others do it as a part of their normal sales cycle.

If you're in a bind and need some cash fast, then holding a firesale is probably one of your best options. Of course, if it were easy or obvious how to do this, then everyone would do it successfully; and there would be no need for a guide such as this one. But this isn't the case. Here's what I personally suggest you do to ensure that your firesale is successful:

Step #1: Pick a Demographic Before You Start

Before you even begin, it's a good idea to pick a demographic to sell to. If you don't know who your target audience is before you get started, then it will be impossible for you to select the right things to sell to them; and it will also be impossible for you to pitch to them in a relatable way.

Step #2: Develop a Truly Attractive Firesale Package

If you currently have a large product line, then this stage shouldn't be terribly challenging for you. All you'll have to do is select a handful of your products, bundle them together, and then sell them for a fraction of the normal cost.

On the other hand, if you don't have your own product line, then this part could be a little more challenging. You'll have to actively seek out products that offer some type of resale license, bundle them together, and then sell them at a tiny fraction of the normal combined price.

Step #3: Compute the Savings

Once you've assembled a large package of goods and have selected the firesale price, spend some time to determine how much it would cost an individual buyer to assemble all of these products (with normal—not resale—licenses). You can then present this figure repeatedly in all of your advertisements.

Step #4: Pitch Your Firesale

Again, if you have your own product line, website, and autoresponder list, then this step will be relatively easier. In this case, you should start by pitching your firesale to your existing customers. As an added incentive, you might offer to make it even cheaper for people on your email list.

A good place to start is by creating a salespage for your firesale. Be careful to detail exactly how much buyers will save, so that they understand exactly how good the deal is. Also, include full descriptions of every product they will have access to after buying.

If you don't feel comfortable writing copy, that's perfectly fine. You can always hire someone from Elance to write the copy for you. Alternatively, you can spend some time on copywriting forums; and look for people who are marketing their services there. These individuals are more likely to have a strong background in marketing principles and copy-writing in particular (whereas those on Elance may be good writers, but not know much about marketing).

Once you have a salesletter, your next step should be to make a pitch to your email list. This will require you to write some short email copy. Here, you will just want to be brief, avoid the appearance of spam, and keep the tone of a letter. A good approach is usually to say something like the following:

==============

[Name],

I don't usually do this, but I'm holding a firesale this week. I'm going to sell my entire line of products for a mere 10% of the normal price. The catch is that I'm only going to allow people to buy at this price on Friday. If you want a chance to get in on this incredible deal, I suggest that you check out what I'm offering at [firesale URL] and make sure to come back on Friday.

I guarantee you won't be disappointed.

Yours,
[Name]

==============

Again, the idea is to avoid something that appears too overtly salesy. Instead, you want to pitch it casually as an opportunity, but with a time limit and an associated sense of urgency.

On the other hand, if you don't already have a list and a line of products of your own, it's still a good idea to start by creating a salesletter; however, your approach here should probably be different.

One good way to create a firesale salesletter for products that are not your own is to setup countdown clock on the page; and then incrementally add the items that will be part of your sale over time. For instance, on day one, you could add three pieces of software that will be included in the firesale to the page. On day two, you could add a bundle of 200 ghostwritten articles that will be included. And so on.

The goal of this exercise should be to get people in the habit of returning to your site daily, so that your firesale successfully builds anticipation until the final night, when your sale will begin. By this time, if you did a good job, hundreds of people will have seen your sale; and will be ready to buy.

As far as the actual promotional process goes, you have several options if you don't already have a mailing list:

1.   Adwords. Since your goal is to raise money fast and since the firesale will only be available for a limited window of time, Adwords is probably one of your best options when it comes to marketing. Remember to use multiple campaigns, to carefully write your text ads, and to limit each campaign to narrowly-focused set of keywords and keyphrases.

2.   Joint Ventures. Find other business owners who have large, active lists. Offer them a very high commission if they participate (i.e. on the other of 50% or 75% of each sale). This will not only help you from the sales that they bring in directly, but it will help you indirectly by raising your status by association.

3.   Post on Forums. While most forums will prohibit you from directly marketing your products through a thread, most will allow you to include a signature that markets your products. You can do this in all large, relevant forums that you frequent; and when you do, make sure that you include the date of the firesale in your signature, so that forum members gain a sense of urgency.

Summary

A firesale can be one of the easiest ways to make money fast online; however, if you don't manage it correctly, you could find yourself spending hundreds of dollars on products without any real return to speak of.

Method #2: Find a Freelance Tutoring Job

Much like finding a babysitting job, finding a tutoring job is another excellent way to make money fast. Not only is possible to get a job that starts tonight, but there's also a good chance that you'll get paid in cash on the spot. And when you're in a bind, it doesn't get much better than that.

When it comes to tutoring, there's a good chance that the student or the student's parents will want you to have some sort of formal credentials. In some cases, they'll simply want you to be in college. In other cases, they'll want you to have a bachelor's degree or an advanced degree. And in other cases, they'll want you to have significant prior teaching and/or tutoring experience.

If you're already starting to worry that your credentials may not be sufficient, don't. If you satisfy even one of the criteria, there's a good chance you'll be able to find a bunch of tutoring gigs; and then leverage them into future gigs (if you decide to continue with it).

Before you do anything else, start by creating a resume that focuses on skills that you have that are pertinent to tutoring. This should include all prior teaching and tutoring experience, all degrees you hold, all standardized tests scores (if relevant), all reference you have from past tutoring work you have done, and all relevant coursework you have done on the collegiate level.

Once you finish typing up your resume in Word, spend some time to format it so that it looks nice, and then save it in PDF format. Whenever you send out applications for prospective tutoring jobs, you should always attach a copy of your resume.

Now that everything is prepared, your next step is to look for tutoring jobs online. Again, you can do this through www.care.com and www.collegehelpers.com (if you are in college). Another great source of tutoring jobs is www.craigslist.org.

If you do decide to search for tutoring jobs through www.craigslist.org, one thing you'll notice is that many of the tutoring jobs are posted by agencies. If you want to continue to do tutoring in the long term, working through an agency may be your best option. If you're looking for short-term work agencies may not be your best option, as they are unlikely to pay in cash; and will require you to do through a lengthy application process.

On the other hand, if you do want longer term jobs, you should seek out all of the agency jobs and post an application on each agency website.

Method #3: Sell Junk Online

If you're like most people, you probably have a lot of junk sitting your house that you have no use for. You might have an old computer or laptop, old electronics, old furniture, old textbooks, and old clothing.

As far as you're concerned, this stuff is useless. You won't ever use it again; and all it's doing is taking up space. But for many other people, they would be willing to pay for an old computer, old furniture, or old clothes.

Once you realize this, you'll also see that selling junk that you no longer use could been an excellent way to raise some cash without too much work.

In the past, if you wanted to do this, you'd have to hold a garage sale; and would have to advertise for it by posting signs on telephone poles all over your neighborhood. If you were lucky, a handful of people would show up and pay very little for some of your stuff. But this is no longer the case.

Now, you can use two important tools to ensure that you get a higher price and also close the sale faster: www.craigslist.org and www.ebay.com. For things like clothing and light electronics, www.ebay.com is probably a better option. It is a thicker market; and will allow you to unload just about everything you have if you're willing to sell at a low enough price.

On the other hand, www.craigslist.org is good if you're selling heavy items, such as furniture. Since shipping would be prohibitively expensive for most furniture, it simply does not make sense to do it on www.ebay.com. If you use www.craigslist.org instead, there's a good chance you'll be able to find someone in your area who will be willing to drive to your house or apartment to pick up the item.

When it comes to using either www.ebay.com or www.craigslist.org, it's important that you spend time to briefly explain what it is you are selling, so that potential buyers know what you're offering. It is also important to include pictures of the items you're selling, as doing this will make browsers significantly more willing to buy.

Method #4: Sell Crafts on Etsy

If you're an artistic person, selling your wares on www.etsy.com/ might be a good option if you're looking to raise cash quickly. If you're unfamiliar with the site, it's a place where artisans can sell various homemade goods in a thick, online marketplace.

Some important things to note about Etsy are the following: 1) everything you sell must be something you made yourself; 2) it costs 20 cents to list an item for 4 months; and 3) each sale will incur a 3.5% transaction fee.

As far as what you can sell on Etsy goes, hot sellers include pieces of art, bags and purses, candles, toys for children, crocheted items, holiday decorations, quilts, vintage pieces, and wedding decorations.

For a basic overview of the "dos and don'ts" of selling on Etsy, you should view the guide they've placed online here: http://www.etsy.com/dosdonts.php.

While there are many ways to make money with Etsy, the experts suggest that building items around a single theme and specializing is one of the best ways to get noticed and to sell items. This is usually a better option that creating a lot of disparate items in different categories.

Overall, Etsy provides a good opportunity to make money online fast; and while doing something you enjoy already. However, if you're not particularly artistic or don't have an interest in crafts, then Etsy may not be a good option for you.

Method #5: Sell Your Own Special Reports… The Fast Way

As I said in the introduction, my goal in this e-book is not to tell you how to build a business. I want to tell you how to make money immediately. If you end up with a successful business as a byproduct, then that's just a bonus.

With that said, it's important to realize that online businesses don't usually turn a profit overnight. Instead, it is usually a long process that will only turn a profit after months have passed.

There are two general reasons why online businesses usually don't turn a profit quickly. The first is that many Internet-based business owners have little or no formal training; and often make serious errors in the implementation stage. And the second reason is that good long-term business plans generally require you to gradually promote your site through things like search engine optimization, cross-promotional agreements, and joint ventures.

While these long-term techniques are essential for business plans, they won't work to make you money tonight. If you want to make money tonight, you essentially have two options: 1) you can use PPC advertising; or 2) you can use word-of-mouth advertising. Other than that, it is unlikely that other techniques will yield immediate sales.

With that said, let's breakdown the process step-by-step, so that you can understand how to make a quick profit with this technique.

Step #1: Create Your Product… Fast

When it comes to writing a special report, don't be a perfectionist. Spend no more than a half hour to come up with your topic. Once you've done that, spend no more than two hours researching the topic. And once you've done that, spend no more than five hours to write the report.

When you're done with the whole process, stop working on your report for the night. Come back to it the following day, edit it thoroughly, format it, and then create a PDF version. Even though your goal is to do everything quickly, you should make sure that it is error-free, well written, and contains useful information.

Additionally, as a general rule, you should pick a topic you're already familiar with. If you're familiar with Internet marketing, write a report about Internet marketing. If you're a good cook, write a report about cooking. If you know something about buying cars, then write a guide about that.

Whatever you do, make sure that you come up with a catchy hook for your product. There should be something about your special report that others will find interesting; and that will draw them to buy. With the vast amount of free information widely available on the Internet, it is critical to be able to market your product in a way that differentiates from everything else available.

Once you complete your product, it's time to move on to the site-building phase.

Step #2: Build Your Site… Quickly

Again, the point of this exercise is to get your product made and put in front of as many buyers as quickly as possible. This means that you can't take your time when it comes to the site-building phase.

I personally suggest that you register a domain, purchase cheap hosting, and immediately install a plug-in that will allow you to edit your site using a what-you-see-is-what-you-get (WYSIWYG) editor. Most hosting sites will offer a large variety of these editors, but I suggest using something simple and something that offers a lot of different templates. Wordpress is probably a good option.

Once you've installed the WYSIWYG editor, it's time to select a good sales page template. Your choice should be clean, professional, and free of distractions, such as links to other pages.

After you do that, it's time to put up a salesletter. Again, time is of the essence, so don't bother with long-copy. Keep it short, sweet, and to the point. Make sure you have a good hook, a number of bullet points that highlight the products benefits (rather than features), and a call to action (to buy).

Finally, add a PayPal payment button. If you want to ensure that you make sales immediately, it's a good idea to keep the price low (say, between $3 and $7). This will ensure that you maintain a high conversion rate.

Step #3: Advertise

Once you have a functioning sales page, a product to sell, and check-out system, it's time to begin advertising your product. However, in this case, it's a good idea to skip SEO and slow promotional methods—and move immediately to PPC and word-of-mouth advertising.

As far as PPC advertising goes, this is as simple as creating a Google Adwords account and making several advertising campaigns. Remember to focus each campaign narrowly. Also, remember to use the root keyword in your campaign multiple times in your advertisement, so that it shows up in bold when people see your ad.

Finally, once you have your PPC campaign working, consider using some word-of-mouth channels to spread the word about your product. If you are a member of online forums related to your product's niche, you should include a link to your salespage in your signature; and make an effort to post frequently, so that others see it. You should also consider offering a deal to members of the forum.

Conclusion

If you want to make cash fast, selling your products online is always a good option; however, you cannot do it using the conventional formula for Internet business creation. Instead, you have to cut out all obstacles that will slow down payments, slow down traffic flows, and generally prevent you from realizing a profit within days.

Using the template I've given above, you should be able to make money within days, as long as you push yourself to stick to the timeline I've suggested.

Method #6: Freelance as an Administrative Assistant

One easy way to raise some cash fast is to work as an administrative assistant. Usually, this means doing things like record-keeping, database entry, and other repetitive tasks; however, in other situations, it might mean something like submitting links to directories, managing an affiliate program, or something like that.

Whatever the case may be, the only requirement is usually that you be good with computers and with the Microsoft Office suite of products. Other than that, you will probably be given a detailed set of instructions that explain exactly what you should be doing on a daily basis.

When looking for administrative assistant jobs, a good place to look is www.elance.com. If you need immediate payment, you should look for one-time, small jobs. Put in a low bid; and offer to work around the clock until you complete it. If you do a good job, there's a chance the client will release the funds to you within days, which you can then transfer to your PayPal account.

Alternatively, you can pick up very large jobs; and require clients to make a deposit of, say, 30% on acceptance of your bid. This means that you will get 30% of the project's full cost as soon as you are hired, which you can immediately transfer to your PayPal account and then deposit in your bank.

As a final note, one key to doing well with these types of projects is to make credible bids. You can do this by writing a proposal that is specifically tailored to the project, rather than just writing something generic. You can also do this by submitting samples of your relevant work, a copy of your resume, and anything else that might provide pertinent information to the job poster.

Method #7: Become a Freelance Writer

Before we get into this one, it's important to keep in mind that freelance writing is not for everyone. If, today, you don't feel comfortable with your writing skills, then using them to make money is perhaps not the best way to go. Even if you work very hard, it is unlikely that you will be able to transform your skills significantly enough to make money with your writing in the short run. In the long run, however, this might be a viable strategy.

On the other hand, if you feel comfortable with your writing, then freelancing is an excellent way to make money fast online. With that said, let's take at your two major options when it comes to sources of freelance writing jobs.

Sites for Freelancers

If you decide to become a freelance writer, there are two important sites you should join: www.guru.com and www.elance.com. These sites allow freelancers to post bids on tens of thousands of writing, translation, graphic design, programming, and administrative assistant projects.

Although you can join both sites for free, you will quickly see why it is a good idea to upgrade your account for at least one of the sites. Upgrading will enable you to bid on more categories of projects and also to bid on more projects within each category. It will also demonstrate your credibility to project posters.

If you decide to upgrade your Elance account, you may want to consider adding the "writing and translation" category, as well as the "marketing and advertising" category. Even though "marketing and advertising" includes many non-writing projects, it includes things such as special report-writing, salesletter-writing, and ad-writing. If you're a good writer and have a background in IM, you'll be especially well suited to these types of jobs.

When using Elance and Guru, it is important to note that individuals with good reputations tend to receive the most projects. And there's a good reason for this: they have the most credibility; and this is what project posters want in freelancers.

When you first start off, there's little you can do to immediately project credibility. So, if you want to compete, you will have to do it along other margins—namely, price and completion time. If you can offer low prices and fast delivery times, there's a good chance you'll get selected every once in a while.

Another important thing to keep in mind is that you will not be selected for most of the projects you bid on. In fact, when you start, you can expect to get rejected at least 75% of the time. Don't use this as a reason to give up. Instead, continue to post on all projects that seem reasonable, given your skills; and get comfortable with the idea that you won't always be selected. As you complete more projects and get more feedback, your acceptance rate will improve.

As a final note, it is always a good idea spend some time sorting through projects before you settle on any one in particular. Personally, I would recommend browsing through all relevant projects closing within 2-3 days. Each time you find one that looks good to you, add it to your watch list. When you have completed this process, go back and look at each project carefully. Take a look at the high and low bids, the promised completion times of the other bidders, and the work involved. Decide whether it's something you can do well; and, if so, whether you could complete it at a competitive price and within a reasonable amount of time.

If you decide that all of your criteria are satisfied, then bid on the project. By the end of the process, you will probably bid on multiple projects at the same time, but keep in mind that most will reject you, anyway, so this is unlikely to be a problem.

If you want to ensure that your bids have a high chance of being successful, then you should spend time reading the project description and writing a good, detail-oriented proposal. Most project posters won't selected a generic proposal, but instead will opt for a proposal that demonstrates that the bidder was paying attention to the project, has the relevant skills, and can make a case for his being able to do the work described.

Of course, there's a lot more you can do with freelancing sites, but for now, I will leave it at that. If you want to make cash with them fast, you should immediately begin implementing the steps I've mentioned above.

Craigslist.org

There's no need for a detailed description here. Finding freelancing jobs on Craigslist is relatively simple, since there's no way to receive feedback or develop a reputation through the site. All you have to do is search in the "jobs" and "gigs" sections. Whenever you see something that lines up with your skills, email the poster with a copy of your resume and a brief, but detailed proposal. Try to make a strong case for why you would be the best candidate for the position.

Internet Marketing Forums

Since good marketing involves a lot of writing, Internet marketers often hire freelance writers to complete projects. These projects include things such as e-books, reports, articles, salesletters, text ads, and site content.

There are a number of places where you can connect with Internet marketers to find projects; however, one of the better places is probably on Internet marketing forums, such as www.warriorforum.com. There, you will find tens of thousands of Internet marketers, many of whom need writing done.

Of course, simply showing up and posting on the forum won't necessarily result in your getting jobs. Instead, you will need to make a reputation for yourself, so that marketers begin to actively seek you out as a source for content.

For starters, a good way to get your name out there and circulating among Internet marketers is to demonstrate that you can produce high-quality work in a way that doesn't cost them anything. One way you can do this is to post a special offer in the trade/sales portion of the IM forum. Instead of simply posting a "good deal," offer something that is truly irresistible. For instance, you might offer to write articles for half the going market rate for a limited period of time. This will probably flood you with work, but will be worth it in the long run, as you may gain may new clients.

Finally, remember that your success will be heavily dependent on word-of-mouth advertising among Internet marketers. This means that if you do a poor job on projects, you could permanently damage your reputation; and make it exceedingly hard to get new projects. And, on the other hand, if you do good work, it could reap dividends for years to come.

Method #8: Freelance Graphic Design Work

Similar to freelance writing, freelance graphic design work is an excellent way to make money online and quickly. If you've already done graphic design work of some sort, this is a definite plus; however, if you haven't, don't worry. It's still possible to make money online doing graphic design work.

For now, I will assume that you don't have any prior experience. In that case, it is essential that you begin by accumulating items to put in your portfolio, which you will show to prospective clients. At a minimum, you will want to create the following objects: 1) an e-book cover; 2) a banner; 3) a small business logo; and 4) a payment button.

If you're not skilled with Photoshop (or GIMP, the free analog to Photoshop), this type of work probably won't be easy initially. You'll probably do very poorly on your first few banners, but with a little work, you can get better.

If you plan to sell banners, one good way to start is by going to the following site: http://mybannermaker.com/. This site will allow you to create a banner by uploading a background image, inserting text, and tweaking a few options. It's easy to do; and it is also free.

One good way to approach this process is to edit each component individually in GIMP or Photoshop before you insert it into the banner using http://mybannermaker.com/. Once the editing is finished, the only step that remains is to combine everything using the site.

Remember, since all of your work is likely to be used for commercial purposes, it is critical to use "stock photos" and photos that are in the public domain. Otherwise, you could be violating someone's copyright.

Once you have created a small portfolio of items that are sufficiently attractive and well-polished. It's time to begin marketing your work through various channels. I personally suggest that you use the following three channels.

Channel #1: Elance

As I mentioned earlier, Elance is a good place to pick up freelance writing and editing projects. It is also a good place to find work if you are a freelance graphic designer. All you have to do is post your portfolio in your profile, bid reasonably on projects, and then wait for people to accept. As you gain credibility, your acceptance rate will rise.

Channel #2: Sitepoint.com and Warriorforum.com

Site users at both of these places require a great deal of graphic design work; and if you want to make money as a graphic designer, you should take advantage of this. Start by making an offer people cannot resist. For instance, offer to make site logos for $3 (or free) for one week. If you actually produce high-quality logos, the forums will be buzzing about your work by the end of the week; and future work will come flowing in without your needing to do anything else.

Channel #3: Craigslist.org

As I mentioned earlier, Craigslist is a great place to find freelance writing projects. This is also true for graphic design projects. Just keep in mind that you can search for jobs in any Craigslist city site, since many of them do not require you to work on-location.

Summary

Freelance graphic design work is an excellent way to raise cash quickly; however, it is important to keep in mind that submitting low quality work may very well ensure that you never get a project. So, before you get started, work out all the kinks until you can create an acceptable portfolio. After that, go forward with your work and also ensure that you match or exceed your clients' expectations.

Method #9: Internet Marketing for Local Businesses

If you have any experience with Internet marketing, you probably know a lot more than the average local business owner. In many cases, local businesses do not have websites; and do not actively market their businesses via the Internet.

Local Restaurants

You should take advantage of the knowledge and experience you have to sell Internet marketing services to local businesses. In particular, one good place to start is by selling your services to local restaurants. One thing you might do for local restaurants is offer to get them connected with Internet-based ordering services.

In many places in the U.S., sites like Foodler.com and Grubhub.com allow visitors to order from sites online; however, many local restaurants do not use these sites and many not even know about them. By joining these sites, local businesses have the opportunity to significantly improve the amount of orders they receive; and also to streamline the process by receiving them via the Internet, rather than over the phone.

Your role in this process would be to assist the restaurants in this process. You can do this by offering to setup Foodler.com and Grubhub.com accounts for nominal fee. This would entail collecting information about the restaurant's menu, hours, etc.—and then submitting it to these sites.

After you complete this process, you can offer to market these businesses in other ways. For instance, if they do not have a website, you can offer to create and maintain one for a small fee (perhaps for $200 for the startup, but then $50 per month thereafter). Since these sites are likely to require little maintenance, you can accumulate a large portfolio of sites.

Now, if you're not familiar with web design, do not worry. Without knowing any HTML, you can create a website using a what-you-see-is-what-you-get (WYSIWYG) editor. If you own a Mac, you can use iWeb. If have a PC, you might choose to do this with FrontPage or DreamWeaver. Alternatively, you can do this using a free program, such as http://kompozer.net/ or http://www.w3.org/Amaya/.

Whatever you do, make sure that you spend enough time working with the WYSIWYG editor before you try to do any work for your clients. If you do a very poor job on a site, you can expect your client to be very angry and dissatisfied, since this will be his/her only web presence.

Other Local Businesses

In general, most companies can benefit from a web presence, even if it doesn't gain them any additional new customers. This is why it is a good idea to contact small, local businesses (who have Yellow Pages listings, but not web sites) to offer to help them setup a site.

Of course, you should always prepare in advance before you contact any company. If your sales pitch is weak or ill-informed, there's a good chance you'll be rejected fast. So, start by writing out a standard pitch. In your pitch, make sure you communicate clearly that having a web presence will allow existing customers to gain more information about the company online, which has the potential to increase sales, even if the customer base does not increase.

Finally, consider starting a single site for a given town. On this site, create an index of all businesses that are willing to pay a small fee (perhaps $50/year, initially); and then optimize the site for search engine traffic. On each business's page, place pertinent information about what they do, where they are located, and what they sell.

If you really want to make an impact on the business owner, create a page for their business in advance and put it on your site. When you make the pitch, you can call the owner, ask him to look at the site, and then get back to you about whether he would like to pay the fee to keep his business's listing on your site. Remember, you can do this with many cities and many businesses.

Summary

Frequently, Internet marketers overlook an important group of buyers: local businesses that do not have any web presence. Without even employing cutting-edge techniques, you can help these businesses to gain a web presence while earning a handsome reward in the process.

Method #10: Web Design Work

In the previous section, we discussed one type of web design work that you can do to make money—namely, creating sites for local businesses and creating local business directories. In addition to this, there are other ways that you can make money through web design.

Selling Your Services as a Freelance Web Designer

If you haven't already designed multiple web sites, it's probably not a good idea to try to sell yourself as a high-end web designer. However, as long as you have a WYSIWYG editor, know a little about Internet marketing, and are willing to work hard, you can expect to earn a decent bounty from mid-to-low level web design work.

Since I've gone over the general concept of freelancing several times already, I won't focus on it too much here. Again, look at sites like Elance.com, SitePoint.com, Guru.com, and others when trying to sell your web design services. Additionally, remember that it is vital to have a portfolio (perhaps one site with multiple sub-domains to show off various styles and themes) and to avoid overselling your skills.

Sell Site Re-Designs to Companies

This is a little bit harder than doing typical web design work. Instead of simply selling your services, getting site specs, and then performing the design job, you will need to start this process by seeking out sites (and preferably sites of local businesses) that could benefit from a site-re-design.

Once you have located these sites, make a pitch to the business owner. Offer to redesign the site, so that it is more functional, provides more interactive features for visitors, generates more traffic, and appears more professional and better-organized. When you begin this process, offer to do it for a very low price until you build up a customer base; and begin receiving some feedback.

Another thing you should do is to offer to maintain the site once it is re-designed. This means that you would be on call to monitor downtime; and to make any changes needed. This might seem like a hassle, but it could be well worth it if you accumulate a large portfolio of sites that require very little maintenance. By charging around $50/month for maintenance, you could reap a large and virtually passive income while only working 10-15 hours per week.

Summary

Freelance web design is an excellent way to make money, even if you have only created one or two websites and know nothing about Flash, php, or even html. The key is that you should work with a WYSIWYG editor (and master it over time), focus on working with local businesses, and sell the maintenance work as a package. Additionally, you should make an attempt to pitch your proposal over the phone.

Method #11: Put an Advertisement on Your Car

Another quick way to raise some cash is to have a "wrap" put on your car. If you've never heard of this before, it's basically just large advertisement that is either painted on or attached to your car. Normally, companies will pay to put wraps on their own fleet of cars; however, some companies also choose to advertise by paying normal drivers $300-750 per month to use a wrap that advertises the company's products.

Unfortunately, getting selected for these positions can be difficult. Hundreds or even thousands of drivers often queue up as soon as companies begin offering these opportunities, so it can often be hard to find a spot.

Additionally, if you have a history of moving violations (such as multiple speeding tickets within a short period of time), then you may not be eligible—or at least your application won't be given top priority. You may also not be disqualified if you do not drive frequently or if you don't live in a major population center.

If this still sounds like a good idea to you, you can get specific information about this opportunity at the following sites:

1. http://www.adsmartoutdoor.com/driversreg.htm
2. http://www.ad-wraps.com/driversinfo_signup.htm

If you live outside of the U.S., there are still many other similar advertising opportunities. Just look for mobile advertising companies in your area.

Method #12: Associated Content, Helium, Constant-Content

As I mentioned in earlier sections, working as a freelance writer can be highly lucrative; however, what I did not mention originally is that there are several other possibilities when it comes to freelance writing. You don't always have to look for a buyer; and then create a project that matches her specifications.

Rather, there are other models of freelance writing that don't involve you using Elance or forums to find customers. In particular, sites like www.associatedcontent.com, www.helium.com, and www.constant-content.com permit you to participate in such alternative freelancing approaches.

Within this class of sites, there are two important additional categories: 1) the category of sites that facilitate direct sales of your writing; and 2) the category of sites that permit you to post content—and then pay you according to how frequently it is viewed on the site.

Category 1 Sites

Sites like www.associatedcontent and www.constant-content.com will permit you to post articles on their site. Publishers will then browse the site for topics of interest; and purchase your articles if they think it would be a good match for their site's content.

One benefit of using this category of freelance site is that your articles will usually sell for a high price (i.e. for $15-20/each, rather than $5/each). Additionally, if you truly enjoy writing, the higher prices will permit you to create something requires research and careful thought, rather than something that simply requires you to write as quickly as is possible.

The major downside of this type of freelancing is that there's no guarantee that anyone will buy your articles at the end of the day. This means that you could invest hours in your articles; and could ultimately never make any money.

Category 2 Sites

Unlike category 1 sites, category 2 sites, such as www.helium.com, do not match you with a buyer. Instead, you give the site your content; and, in return, you gain revenue whenever someone views your article. Usually, this amounts to something like 1-3 cents per view.

In general, if you plan to use category 2 sites, you should be careful about which topics you pick. Since these sites usually generate revenue through Google AdSense, they often pay accordingly. This means that you should write about topics that businesses spend a lot of advertising money on.

It might not initially be obvious what these topics are, but if you spend some time on Google Adwords searching for keywords, you should be able to scrape together some keywords that people pay a great deal to advertise for.

Summary

Ultimately, neither of these methods provides a lighting-fast way to make money. If you need money today or by the end of the week, you definitely have other options that are better (such as using Elance.com or Guru.com to find freelancing projects); however, as a form of supplementary income, these sites are not a bad option.

Method #13: Find a Freelance Babysitting Job

If you're tired of reading guides that supposedly will teach you how to make money online—but do little other than belch hot air about some business opportunity—then this method will come as a breath of fresh air to you.

Instead of creating a website, building traffic over time, creating a product, and then waiting for the profits to flow in, you can simply look for a babysitting job that will likely pay you cash (and possibly even the same day).

Today, the process of getting a babysitting job isn't the same as it was 10 years ago. You don't need to know someone who knows someone who needs a babysitter. All you have to do is locate good places online to find parents who need babysitters; and then submit dozens of job applications. In a matter of hours, you very well could have a job lined up for tonight.

Start by going to www.care.com. This is one of the best places to find sitting jobs. All you have to do there is create a profile, and do a good job of advertising yourself. Remember to highlight things about yourself that will put potential employers at ease; and will communicate to them that you will be good sitter.

In addition to this, there are two other things you may want to consider doing: 1) allowing www.care.com to run a background check on you, so that you can demonstrate to parents that you do not pose any threat to the children. Also, you may want to consider including a picture of yourself in your profile, so that your application has a more human feel to it.

In addition to www.care.com, there are many other places for you to locate sitting jobs. One of those places is www.craigslist.org. You can start by going to the site and then selecting the major city closest to your place of residence.

Once you have done this, browse and search through the "gigs" and "jobs" section to locate promising sitting jobs. Look for parents who are willing to pay cash; and who need a sitter immediately (perhaps because they have plans for the evening). Since they will have fewer options and will be in a rush, there's a better chance they'll select you and do so without taking up a lot of your time with interviews, questions, and other formalities.

Overall, this strategy is an excellent way to make cash fast when you're in a bind. This is especially true if you have past sitting experience or have had children of your own.

Method #14: Use Myspace Forums to Sell Products

Social media has proven itself to be one of the best venues for marketing products in a hurry. In the past, Internet marketers have held contests to see how much they can make in one day, one week, or one month by creating a new product and selling it through a social marketing medium.

When it comes to this type of project, there are two things to ask yourself: 1) what type of product should you sell? And 2) what medium should you sell it in? In this section, I will cover how to sell on Myspace forums. In the next section, we'll consider Twitter. Let's start with the types of products you might want to sell on Myspace.

What Product to Sell

You might immediately assume that you should sell one of your flagship products, but in fact, social media sites are not always the best place to do this. For this reason, you will want to answer this question by doing market research, rather than simply picking a product and running with it.

One way you can approach this is to begin browsing through a variety of Myspace member forums. Do this for various categories; and make an attempt to gauge how large the forum following is. Are there hundreds of people who post regularly? Thousands? What is it that they're talking about;

and what information could they possibly need to help them in their endeavors?

Once you find a group that strikes you, begin reading up on their topic of choice; and then participate in the forum discussions. Try to make friends and be helpful. This will benefit you in the long run, since they are unlikely to respond well to you if they perceive you as a green-eyed infiltrator whose only interest is in selling them stuff.'

After you have a feel for the forum and the topic, commission a writer through a site like Elance to create a powerful, but brief, "how to" manual on some specific facet of their topic. For instance, you might follow a jewelry group; and decide to create a guide on how to purchase high quality beads online at a steep discount.

Whatever you do, make sure that this topic is something you hear about on the forum frequently. Your goal should be to provide a product that solves a problem that seems to be common among forum members.

Once you have this guide in hand, create a mini-site with a short copy salespage; and a PayPal checkout button, so that you can receive payment immediately. On the salesletter, highlight the following benefits of your guide:

- Explain how it will tangibly improve the lives of your target demographic group (i.e. after you read my guide, you will be able to do task x twice as fast) in general.

- Highlight the specific benefits of certain chapters (i.e. chapter 8 alone will save you $100 per month).

Also, consider selling your guide for a very, very low price. Your goal here should be to make the decision to purchase a no-brainer. At least initially, you shouldn't bludgeon your new customers with high-end products. Introduce them to your work with something that costs around $3-7. If you do a good job with everything else, you could easily make around $500 in a matter of days.

The final step is market your product by creating a signature that references it. Beyond that, all you can do is post frequently; and hope that people see it and buy.

Method #15: Use Twitter to Market Your Myspace Forum Product

If you used method #14, you now have an inexpensive, entry-level product, a sales page, and a check-out system. All you need to do now is direct additional traffic to it. While posting on Myspace Forums was a good way to start, there are still a lot of options available for traffic generation.

One such option is Twitter. If you're unfamiliar with Twitter, it's a social networking service that allows you to add and remove friend as you would on Myspace or Facebook. The difference is that the main purpose of Twitter is to send out 140-character "tweets" to your friends; and, in return, to read what they are tweeting about.

Of course, this network can also be used to make money. To do this, you'll need to start by creating an account if you do not already have one. After that, you will want to begin adding people who might be good targets for your sales campaign. You can do this by searching to see who is tweeting about topics related to your product. You can then add them.

After a week or so, if you worked diligently, you will have hundreds of followers. What you should do next is begin making tweets that do not directly pitch your product.

Instead, they should simply communicate interesting and useful information about your product niche.

Your goal in this whole process is to spur some interest in your twitter profile, which is where you will place a link to your salespage. That's right: instead of using your profile to conduct a massive pitchfest, you will use it to draw people in naturally, so that they view your profile on their own terms— and then decide whether to buy.

Method #16: Enter into a Joint Venture Partnership

If you don't already have a site and an email list of your own, a joint venture can be one of the best ways to make money quickly. When it comes to joint venture partnerships, there are three things to keep in mind:

1. Most good JV partners will reject you initially. If a person immediately accepts your JV offer, there's a good chance that she is not receiving many offers. On the other hand, if she doesn't respond initially or tells you that she'll need more time or a better offer, this probably (but doesn't always) mean that a lot of people are pursuing her as a JV partner.

   Why is this important to understand? Because you will get rejected many times initially when you first begin sending out offers. It is important to understand that partnerships can often be a numbers game; and that you shouldn't be discouraged too easily.

2. Be courteous and make a generous offer. Often, the simple presence of a JV partner will boost your sales and your profile as a marketer far beyond what it will do for you in direct sales from that partner. For this reason, it is always a good idea to approach JV partners with a generous offer; and to be patient, kind, and courteous.

3. Stay focused in your presentation. If you're looking for a JV partner who can drive traffic to your site; and you are willing to offer a profit-sharing arrangement in exchange, then say that upfront. Make sure they understand exactly what it is that you need from them; and exactly what they will get for participating.

If you do these three things—and if you remain persistent—you have a good chance of finding at least a few JV partners who will be willing to work with you and promote your project.

Method #17: Offer Services to Internet Marketers

As an Internet marketer, you understand the sales process. You know how to create ad campaigns, exchange links, create salesletters, manage autoresponders, create check-out pages—and all the other things that Internet marketers do on a daily basis.

As it turns out, this can be very useful if you're in a bid and need cash. You can simply offer your services to Internet marketers on forums and in other places in exchange for small fees. For instance, if you need to make $50/day for the next week, then offer to submit a site's link to 50 directories for $5. You should have no problem pulling in 10 sales per day with that a strategy like that.

Method #18: Offer a Special Offer on the WarriorForum or SitePoint

Several large forums allow members to submit special offers to other members. If you need cash badly, consider using this section on one of the larger Internet marketing forums to sell something that a lot of people need for very cheap.

For instance, consider writing a 15-page report on a current hot topic; and selling it for $3 per copy as a special offer. This may sound like a tiny amount—and indeed it is—but that's exactly the point. You're not selling a massive, comprehensive set of encyclopedias. You're simply selling something small and targeted for a tiny price, so that potential buyers don't have to think hard about what to do.

If you do a good job with this approach and create a valuable product, there's a good chance you'll make hundreds of dollars from your offer.

Warrior Forum – WarriorForum.com

SitePoint – Sitepoint.com

Method #19: Sell Custom Content Mini-Sites

If you can write well and can also do basic graphic design work, consider churning out some custom content mini-sites. This might consist of something like a standard graphics package for a site, including a logo and banners; as well as a 10-15 articles.

Once you have created your content mini-site, consider how best to sell it. Usually, the best place to sell it is a marketing forum; however, the price and the number of copies you want to sell may be harder question. If you believe you can make two sites per day, then it may make sense to sell them for as little as $30/each. Remember, also, that you should research the topics you pick in advance, so that the sites you create will target lucrative keywords for your buyers.

Method #20: Make a 5/95 JV Offer

If you're really desperate and need cash fast, then it may be time to start trying to solicit the help of others more aggressively. One way to do this is to make offers that they cannot refuse. For instance, you could offer to develop a product independently and at your own expense (and also agree to revise it until the JV partner finds it acceptable) if your partner will give you a mere 5% split of the profits she receives from promoting it.

 While it might seem like you're giving away too much here for it to be worth it, this can often be one of your best options when you're in a bind. If even one marketer with a large list accepts this offer, you have the potential to make hundreds—if not thousands—of sales. This could translate into you making several hundred dollars in the span of two weeks.

Method #21: Sell Unprofitable Parts of Your Business

If you already have an Internet-based business, but parts of it aren't performing particularly well, then it may be a good idea to sell off the unprofitable parts, consolidate everything that is working; and move forward with a new model.

These unprofitable sections of your business might include websites that are poorly monetized; or products that don't seem to sell very well. Whatever the case may be, consider selling it on a forum like SitePoint. If you have monthly revenue data (from AdSense or PayPal records), this will be helpful.

Even if the site doesn't sell well for you, that doesn't mean it can't for someone else. This is something that is important to highlight when making the sale. Point out the positives about the site (such as its daily unique visitor counts); and then mention how this can potentially make more money if monetized better.

One good thing about selling your unprofitable sites is that you can usually get something like 7-10 months worth of profit from the sale. Even if your site was making a meager $100/mo, this could translate into an immediate sale for $700-1000.

As far as e-books, reports, and unprofitable intellectual property go, consider selling them on forums. Do whatever you need to in order to make the most from them—whether it be selling the master resale rights; or simply selling them to many people with a restrictive license.

Conclusion

When most Internet marketers talk about making money online, they talk about it in the context of doing it quickly or immediately. In general, this doesn't work if you want to create a viable, long-term business model. However, if you just want to make some cash now and don't care about how stable and scalable your methods are in the long run, there are ways to do it.

In this guide, I've outlined 21 ways to do exactly that: to make money offline or online fast; and without necessarily having any interest in continuing to do so in the long run. If you settle on a handful of these options, take my advice, and work hard, you'll make that money you need for now; and once you have it, you'll be able to return to your long term business plans.

Resources

Site 1 – www.WarriorForum.com

Site 2 – www.Sitepoint.com

Site 3 – www.helium.com

Site 4 – www.associatedcontent.com

Site 5 – www.twitter.com

Site 6 – www.flippa.com

Site 7 – www.autoblogblueprint.com